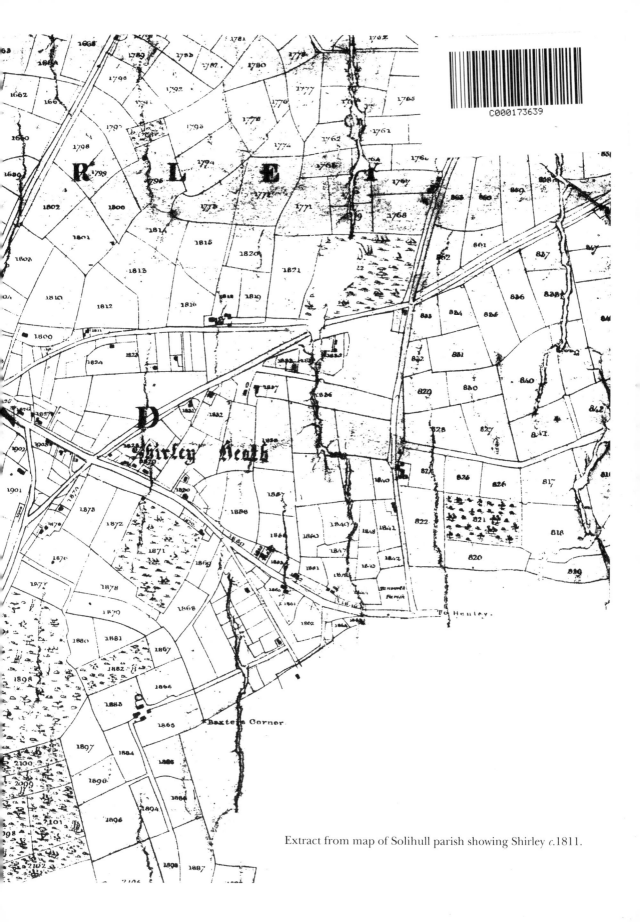

Extract from map of Solihull parish showing Shirley *c.*1811.

SHIRLEY
A Pictorial History

Stratford Road in the 1920s.

SHIRLEY
A Pictorial History

Sue Bates

Phillimore

1993

Published by
PHILLIMORE & CO. LTD.
Shopwyke Manor Barn, Chichester, Sussex

ISBN 0 85033 869 7

Printed and bound in Great Britain by
BIDDLES LTD.
Guildford, Surrey

*This book is dedicated to the memory of
Tom Bragg and Mollie Varley,
who both contributed so much
to preserving the history of Shirley.*

List of Illustrations

Frontispiece: Stratford Road in the 1920s.

Illustration Acknowledgements

Miss. C. Adderley, 121; Mr. Arculus, 85; Mrs. Helen Ball, 119; Baptist church, 53-56; Sue Bates, 88, 112, 149, 167; Gordon Bragg, 108, 116-117, 136, 140-141; Mrs. Causer, 11; Mr. T. Clark, 130; Mr. George, 69; Mr. Hodeston, 113; Mrs. F. Knight, 128, 151; John Marks 6, 8, 12, 16, 18-20, 22, 26, 29, 33, 44-45, 129, 131, 142, 156, 162, 164, 165-166, 168, 174, 176-177; Methodist church, 62, Ordnance Survey, 1, 158; Our Lady of the Wayside 63-64; Mrs. Pearse, 69; Progressive Housing Association Ltd, 97; St James' church, 48-50; the late Robert Shaw, 169-170; Shirley Community Association, 111, 137-138; Mrs. D. Smedley, 57-61; Solihull Libraries & Arts, frontispiece, 2-5, 7, 9-10, 13-15, 17, 21, 23-25, 27-28, 30, 32, 34-38, 40-41, 51-52, 66-67, 89-90, 96, 98, 102-103, 105-107, 110, 114-115, 120, 122-124, 133, 135, 143, 147-148. 154-155, 159, 163, 171-173, 175; Mrs. Stanley, 164; Mr. F. W. S. Stokes, 101, 144; Ken Stokes, 145-146; Miss Sunderland, 100; Mr. Tustin, 125-126; Mrs. D. Webb, 39, 47, 152; the Women's Institute, 31, 42-43, 46, 65, 68, 70-84, 86-87, 91-95, 99, 104, 109, 127, 132, 134, 153, 157, 160-161; Mrs. J. Woodall, 150.

Acknowledgements

I would like to record grateful thanks to all those who have helped me to prepare and research this work, including the following: Gordon Bragg, Mrs. Margaret Causer, Mr. T. Clark, Mrs. Frances Knight, John Marks, Mrs. Dinah Smedley, Shirley Community Association, Shirley Women's Institute, Mr. Tustin, and all the churches in Shirley for loan of their photographs and help with information. Thanks also to Dr. Bob McKee, Director of Libraries & Arts, for allowing me access to the material in the Local Studies Collection at Solihull Library. I am most grateful to several people who have recorded memories of the village for me, including Mr. and Mrs. Hodeston, Mr. Rabin, Miss Rose Vernon, Mr. Tom Warner and Mrs. Wheatcroft. Photographic work has been done by June Lawrence; thanks are also due to Jean Ward for additional research, and to John Bates for help and support.

Finally, I would like to pay tribute to the work done by Shirley Women's Institute in the 1950s and '60s under the leadership of the late Mollie Varley, and to the work done by the late Tom Bragg in collecting information – without their foresight much of the history of the village would have been lost.

Introduction

Shirley was originally part of the parish of Solihull, and previously part of the Manor of Ulverlei. Ulverlei was created in the Anglo-Saxon period and was a large manor stretching from the present Olton across to Solihull in the east, with a long section extending south through Shirley to Dickens Heath. The manor was in the Forest of Arden, an ancient area of woodland covering much of north-west Warwickshire. Solihull, some two miles from Shirley, was created in the 12th century by the lords of the manor of Ulverlei.

An Iron-Age hillfort known as Berry Mound is situated south of Solihull Lodge, to the west of Stratford Road and overlooking the river Cole. This was probably the earliest habitation in the area, which was covered in woodland – as late as the 16th century Solihull Lodge was described as 'Solihull Wood'.

Shirley was situated on the boundary between Worcestershire and Warwickshire, which also represented the boundary between the lands of the tribes of Saxons and Angles respectively. The name 'Shirley' has been given two possible meanings: 'boundary clearing' or 'bright clearing'. Either meaning would seem appropriate. There is also a problem with the exact meaning of the word 'leah', dating from the mid-eighth to mid-tenth centuries, for it can mean 'glade or clearing', 'pasture' and 'meadow'. Dr. Margaret Gelling, writing in *The West Midlands in the early Middle Ages* (published in 1992 by Leicester University Press), states that the use of 'leah' is a reliable indicator of the presence of ancient woodland, that the sense of 'clearing' is the most common meaning, and most likely when names ending in 'leah' are found occurring together in clusters.

The settlement grew up along a trackway through the forest which became known as Shirley Street; this has led to speculation that it was a Roman road because such roads were often given the name 'Street'. There is no documentary evidence to support this theory, however, and the first recorded use of 'Shirley Street' is in 1322. One of the oldest sections of Shirley would seem to be the junction of Stratford Road with Olton Lane and Haslucks Green Road. By the Elizabethan period Olton Lane was known as Cock Lane, and a cluster of buildings at the crossroads, including the old *Cock Inn*, is shown on old maps. The headquarters of the Manor of Ulverlei was at Olton, and this could have been part of a route linking Ulverlei with Bromsgrove and Droitwich (where salt was mined). The route would probably then have continued to Worcester, which was an important trading centre at that time.

Most of the hamlet grew up along the Stratford Road, with farms scattered in the surrounding area. Robert Pemberton, writing in *Solihull and its Church* (1905), commented that settlements in forest areas often developed as a single street (like Henley-in-Arden) with solitary farms and cottages scattered about the area. Solihull was the administrative centre of the area; the residents of Shirley were forced to travel to markets and fairs and to the parish church in Solihull. Field paths leading from Stratford Road became roads such as Solihull Road, linking Shirley and Solihull.

Shirley was a remote hamlet and no major events seem to have occurred there, although there is a tradition that in 1643 Prince Rupert spent a night at the *Cock Inn* on the way to the Battle of Birmingham. Shirley became one of the administrative areas (known as 'ends') of Solihull parish. William Dugdale, the 17th-century Warwickshire antiquarian, reckoned that there were 48 families in 'Sherley End'. The window tax assessment of 1750 showed 32 householders in Sherley End and 24 in Whitlocks End who were liable for payment. These figures would, of course, exclude small tenements not liable for payment.

In 1725 the Stratford Road became a turnpike road and a tollgate was erected in Shirley Street, almost adjacent to the *Saracen's Head* which, together with the *Red Lion*, flourished as a coaching inn. On the whole, however, Shirley remained an isolated farming community until the late 18th century, with most occupations related to agriculture. At that time 'sportsmen' from Birmingham started to travel out to the village to indulge in unsavoury pursuits such as cock-fighting, dog fights, bull-baiting, bare-knuckle fights and so on. Much of this activity seems to have been centred on the *Plume of Feathers*.

Local residents were far from happy with this situation. In 1829 the Rev. Archer Clive became rector of Solihull, and the residents petitioned him to found a chapel in the village. He agreed to endow a chapel if the villagers would build it. As a result St James' church was erected as a chapel-of-ease in 1832 on land given by Clive's cousin, the Earl of Plymouth (who was Lord of the Manor of Solihull). The original building was a simple chapel in the Early English style. In 1843 Shirley became a separate ecclesiastical parish, and its independent history may be said to have started in earnest. The population of the parish was then 1,100.

The first vicar, appointed in 1843, was the Rev. Nash Stephenson, who had been a curate at Solihull. On 13 October 1857 the vicar was married, and the parish celebrated in some style. A testimonial (consisting of a dinner service and various silver articles) was presented to him, and an address given, in which his parishioners expressed their gratitude for his work in the parish on their behalf. The address and Stephenson's reply were printed, the vicar giving a graphic description of life in the village in the early part of the 19th century:

> In the Address reference has been made to the moral improvement of the people of this parish. Of this cheering fact the proofs are plain and undeniable. No long time since, Shirley bore an unenviable notoriety for all that was bad and vicious. Within my recollection and during the early years of my ministry, Shirley Street had become the last resort of the lovers of brutalising sports. It was here they found congenial companions, and it was here they indulged, with impunity and unloosened, in bull-baiting, and cock-fighting, and pugilistic encounters ... I venture to assert ... that Shirley at the present time is not last in the scale of decency and civilisation, [and] will bear ample comparison with the best ... of the adjacent parishes.

Administratively, Shirley remained part of Solihull, although a number of improvements were made to the village, including the provision of a village school. The first school had opened in 1833, and a new building was erected in 1835, on land given by Miss Caroline Meysey Wigley of Olton Hall, who owned much land in the area. In 1846 Caroline (who by then was Mrs. Archer Clive) gave a further three and a half acres of land to build the first vicarage.

A Baptist community had been established in Shirley since the end of the 18th century, when a meeting was held at the former *Cock Inn*, later known as Pear Tree

Cottage, on the corner of Olton Road. In 1845 a Baptist chapel was erected on the opposite side of the road.

During the 19th century the population of the village increased very gradually. A ratebook of 1806 recorded 71 rateable properties in the area. In 1843 the population of the new parish was 1,100, whilst the census of 1891 showed a total of only 1,465. By 1900 the population was around 1,600, but a period of rapid expansion then occurred as more people moved out of neighbouring Birmingham to escape the overcrowding and pollution. The 1911 census records 2,319 inhabitants, and three years earlier the vicar had said 'We can no longer call ourselves a village'.

Censuses and directories of the 19th century show that the majority of occupations carried out by the inhabitants of Shirley were typical of an agricultural community. In addition to farmers, blacksmiths and wheelwrights, there were saddlers, bricklayers, painters, grocers, butchers and bakers to be found. New, larger houses started to appear in the 1870s. The Turnpike Trust was dissolved in 1872, thereby removing tolls on the Stratford Road.

The increasing population required more public services. Gas had been brought to the village in 1886, due largely to the efforts of the vicar, the Rev. Charles Burd. Birmingham's water supply was extended to Shirley in 1886, and Joseph Cary Richards, the landlord of the *Plume of Feathers*, was invited to perform the ceremony of turning on the supply. Mr. Cary Richards was landlord of the *Plume* for many years, during which time the inn lost its former bad reputation.

Towards the end of the 19th century there were great changes in local government administration. In 1889 Warwickshire County Council was created, and Mr. Harvey Chattock was appointed the first member for Solihull (including Shirley). In 1894 district and parish councils were established, and Shirley Parish Council came into being. Mr. John Hemus of Shirley Farm (opposite the *Saracen's Head*) became the first Shirley representative on Solihull Rural District Council.

In 1903 a Wesleyan Methodist chapel was opened on Stratford Road. In 1908 the railway came to Shirley, after much petitioning by local residents. The station was built in Haslucks Green Road, about a mile from the Stratford Road, and was situated on the line to Stratford-upon-Avon. In 1913 the first village police station was opened on Stratford Road with Sergeant Thomas Clark in charge.

Much of the recreation in the village was provided by events at Shirley Village Institute, founded in 1903. Other amusements were still rural in character, such as clay pigeon shooting, bowling and, in winter, skating on frozen flooded fields. Cycling became very popular, and Shirley residents found a useful source of income in the large numbers of city dwellers who cycled along the Stratford Road at weekends and Bank Holidays en route to Earlswood Lakes. Other travellers came in parties in horse-drawn brakes, or enjoyed a country walk. These visitors, although passing through, provided custom for the village, requiring refreshments and change of horses. Cottage industries grew up with many residents displaying the sign 'TEAS'. An ever-dwindling number of inhabitants can remember the quiet days of the village in the early 20th century; fortunately some memories have been recorded, including one gentleman who described making posies and buttonholes (decorated with fern from a local wood) which, as a boy, he would sell to parties in the horse-brakes for a penny or twopence.

During the First World War many young men left the village, some never to return. A number of German prisoners-of-war were allocated to work on farms in the area. A dramatic event occurred in 1917 when a Zeppelin flew over and dropped a bomb, which fortunately fell in fields behind the *Red Lion*. No injuries were caused, although buildings were shaken and many windows blown out. The end of the war was celebrated in July 1919 with a Peace Day celebration. A large memorial was erected at the gate of St James' parish church to commemorate the 67 men and one woman who had lost their lives.

During the 1920s and '30s many houses were built, attracting new residents to the area. New roads, sometimes forming estates, were constructed. More shops were required to cater for the needs of the growing community, and Stratford Road became a popular choice for their location. Several petrol stations also appeared along the Stratford Road as motor vehicles became more common. Electricity was brought to the village in 1926, and Shirley recreation ground opened the following year. The Odeon cinema opened in 1935 and the Lido in 1936. A public library had operated from a converted house for a few years and, in 1937, a new library was built in Church Road by Warwickshire County Council. In 1929 the wooden Methodist chapel burnt down, and was rebuilt in brick to accommodate the larger congregation. In 1934 a Roman Catholic church was opened in a converted house on Stratford Road dedicated to Our Lady of the Wayside. Both events illustrate the changes in population that were taking place.

In 1931 the population was 7,233, and by 1936 *Kelly's Directory of Warwickshire* described Shirley as 'a small town' (earlier editions had called it a 'village'). More schools were needed to provide education for the growing numbers of pupils. In the 1930s new elementary schools were opened at Haslucks Green and Tidbury Green, and Sharman's Cross senior school was opened, with boys and girls in separate departments.

The Second World War brought the 'blackout', air raids, evacuees, and more prisoners-of-war (this time Italians who worked on farms and repaired roads). There was a local branch of the Home Guard, and a British Restaurant opened in 1942 in a temporary building on the site of the present post office. At the end of the war VE Day and VJ Day were celebrated with street parties and bonfires.

Post-war growth in Shirley was rapid and intensive. Numerous houses were built, including the Cranmore estate, and a housing estate replaced Woollaston's pig farm in Priory Road. There were several self-build schemes such as the Shakespeare Manor development. Industry also increased, with more factories opening in the area, especially along the Stratford Road and the Cranmore Boulevard Estate. More shops, banks and offices appeared along Stratford Road from Haslucks Green Road to Monkspath. Gradually, most of the farmland in the area was replaced with buildings. Lucas Group opened a new research centre in Dog Kennel Lane in 1965, and two years later C.E.G.B. (now Powergen) built the first tower block in Shirley as its headquarters.

There was some change in local government in the post-war period – Solihull Urban District Council (afterwards S.U.D.C.) had been formed in 1932, with part of the former S.R.D.C. leaving the borough. In 1954 Solihull became a municipal borough; Shirley played a prominent part in the proceedings on Charter Day when Princess Margaret visited the borough to present the Charter of Incorporation on behalf of the Queen – the formal ceremony took place in the Odeon cinema, Stratford Road. In 1962 Solihull became a county borough, and this rapid rise through the tiers of local government was a result of the dramatic increase in population.

By 1968 the population of Shirley was estimated at about thirty-five thousand. This huge increase had resulted in several new schools in the post-war years being built including:

– Infants Schools: Burman Road, 1952; Cranmore, 1953; Streetsbrook, 1957; Blossomfield, 1958; Peterbrook, 1963; Woodlands, 1965

– Junior Schools: Shirley Heath, 1954; Peterbrook, 1963; St James, 1965; Widney, 1968 and Our Lady of the Wayside RC school, c.1961

– Senior Schools: Lighthall and a new building for Sharman's Cross Boys.

Housing developments for the elderly were also provided: Elizabeth House opened in 1955 and in 1965 bungalows were built in its grounds. Swallow Meadow home for the elderly was also built in 1965.

A new police station was built in the 1960s on the opposite side of Stratford Road, and various public buildings appeared near the site of the former police station including the post office, the clinic, and the Shirley Centre (completed in 1985).

During the 1980s there was a great deal of redevelopment in Shirley, with buildings such as the Odeon cinema replaced by supermarkets. Large retail outlets such as DIY superstores have also appeared, and many small shops have closed down. Traffic, especially along Stratford Road, has increased in recent years, so that it is now impossible to cross the road except at certain controlled points. The opening of the M42 motorway with an access point at the junction of Stratford Road at Monkspath has increased both business use of the area and traffic. There has been a great deal of development at Monkspath, in the section of Stratford Road dubbed 'The Golden Mile', with office and retail developments, fast-food outlets replacing traditional public houses, a multi-screen cinema and a new business park. The new Cranmore-Widney housing development was built on open countryside, with around five thousand houses constructed in an area from Monkspath to Hillfields and Widney Manor, near Solihull.

1993 is a memorable year in Shirley. The parish church celebrates the 150th anniversary of the foundation of the ecclesiastical parish, and many visitors may be surprised by the changes which have taken place in recent years. The Methodist church also celebrates an event – the opening of the new church to replace the building of 1930, now too small for an increased congregation. In all these celebrations and festivities there will inevitably be much interest shown in Shirley's past, which has often been treated dismissively by authors such as Noel Boston (who described it as 'a straggling village ... [with] little of antiquarian interest'). The staff of Solihull Library make every effort to keep a record of the borough's past in the Solihull Local Studies Collection, but additional information is always most welcome to preserve for posterity.

It is hoped that the following selection of photographs will illustrate at least part of the history of Shirley and its inhabitants, and also perhaps act as a reminder for those old enough to remember 'the village'.

Stratford Road

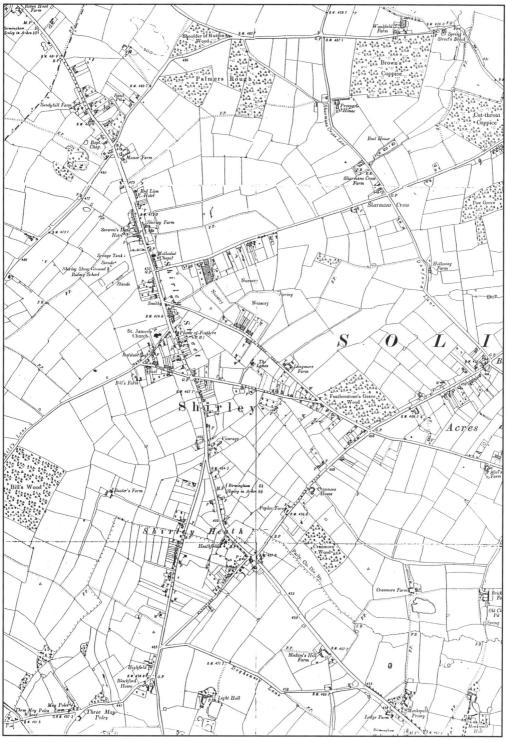

1. The hamlet of Shirley grew along the Stratford Road (known here as Shirley Street). This extract from the second edition Ordnance Survey 6 in. to 1 mile map of 1905 shows the settlement along the former turnpike road. The tollgate had been situated immediately below the *Saracen's Head*. The surrounding area consisted of lanes and fields, with many farms, and several small woods surviving as a reminder that the area was once part of the Forest of Arden.

2. Many photographs exist of Stratford Road taken around the end of the 19th century. This view shows St James' churchyard wall on the left, looking towards the junction with Longmore Road (on the right) in the direction of Birmingham.

3. This view shows the junction of Stratford Road and Church Road, with the cottage which housed the village post office from 1861 to the early 1890s. St James' church is visible on the far side of Church Road.

4.   This photograph shows the section of Stratford Road sometimes called Sandy Hill, *c.*1910. The gate of the original Baptist chapel may be seen on the left, just past the junction with Haslucks Green Road. The cyclists are travelling towards Shirley village. The Powergen building now occupies the site on the left. The cottage which was once the *Cock Inn* stood opposite, on the corner of Olton Road.

5.   The Stratford Road was the turnpike road to London through Stratford and Oxford. The original *Saracen's Head* is shown here on the right, *c.*1913; the large house adjacent was Shirley Lodge. The Shirley tollgate was immediately after Shirley Lodge, with the tollhouse on the opposite side of the road. Tolls ceased in 1872, but the gate remained and was eventually removed to Salter Street Farm at Earlswood.

6. Another view of Shirley Lodge (on the left) and the *Saracen's Head*, looking towards Birmingham. The house was the home and surgery of Dr. J. Coole Kneale until 1935. The site is now an entrance to Shirley Park. Shirley Farm, for many years the home of John Hemus, stood opposite the *Saracen's Head*. This section of the Stratford Road was subject to flooding until quite recently.

7. During the 1920s more shops appeared, such as these shown adjacent to the *Red Lion*. The road surface was still poor, and was often muddy.

8. A study of the large scale Ordnance Survey maps of the Shirley Street area between 1886 and 1918 shows an increase in building along Stratford Road (still referred to as Shirley Street). A view looking south from Knight's post office (left) shows the small collection of shops which for many years formed the nucleus of Shirley village.

9.   The 1930s witnessed a great deal of development in the Shirley area. New houses were built for people moving out of Birmingham, and the Stratford Road became a busier route as motor transport increased.

10. The junction of Tanworth Lane and Stratford Road (looking towards Monkspath) was still fairly rural in character around 1930, when this photograph was taken. For many years this junction was known as Red Cow Corner, named after a former inn.

11. In the 1930s the *Saracen's Head* was rebuilt. This view shows the Stratford Road looking south from the new building, with Shirley Lodge still standing. This photograph was taken from the corner of Stanway Road, one of several new roads created before the Second World War.

12.   More shops and facilities were required to cater for the increased population in the 1930s. This view of Stratford Road, from a postcard dated 1943, shows the rebuilt *Saracen's Head* (centre left) and the changing character of the road.

13.   After the Second World War there was intense development in the surrounding area. Traffic increased, including th provision of more public transport (note the bus stop and shelter on the pavement), thus necessitating brighter and bette street lighting to assist accident prevention. Since the 1950s shops, supermarkets and office developments have appeared along the Stratford Road from Haslucks Green Road to Monkspath, with larger scale projects (especially towards the M42) appearing in the 1980s.

Roads

14.   Many roads lead off the Stratford Road. Several of these were once country lanes, including Bills Lane, shown here in a postcard of *c*.1910. Bills Lane is a continuation of Church Road, and was the site of Bills Farm until its demolition in 1936. There is no documentary evidence for the origin of the name.

15.   Bills Wood, shown here in a postcard of *c*.1905, is typical of the many small woods and coppices in the area, such as Cranmore Wood, Palmer's Rough, Shoulder of Mutton Wood and Featherstone's Grave Wood. As late as the 1950s, a survey showed that the district still contained much woodland (mainly oak, ash and hawthorn) and over 200 species of wild flowers.

16. Haslucks Green was a picturesque hamlet, shown here in an old postcard. The name is first recorded in 1699 in a manuscript in the British Museum and is probably associated with the family of Richard Haseluck (*c*.1580).

17. St James' Place (shown here in 1909) is situated off Church Road adjacent to the churchyard. A gate to the churchyard is shown on the right. The infant school (opened in 1902) can be seen through the trees.

18.   Church Road lies at the side of St James' church and leads to Bills Lane. It was once a quiet road containing trees and cottages, including Church View (now the site of Church House). The new Shirley branch library in Church Road was opened on 5 July 1937, built by Warwickshire County Council. Now operated by Solihull Libraries and Arts, it was extended in 1990.

19.   School Road (shown here *c.*1930) is another side road off Stratford Road. The original village school was built here.

20. Olton Road, seen here *c.*1914, was formerly Cock Lane, and probably a medieval route linking Ulverlei with Bromsgrove and Droitwich via Haslucks Green. The old *Cock Inn* once stood at the corner of Stratford Road, and its unusual carved stone inn sign was later preserved at a local farm.

21. A later view of Olton Road shows houses built to cater for the rising population, as more people moved out of Birmingham to live in the cleaner atmosphere of the surrounding countryside.

22.   Union Road, originally Shirley Heath Road, was created in the 19th century to link Stratford Road with Blossomfield Road. Bronte Farm (now the site of a housing estate) was situated here, and Featherstone's Grave Wood was at the junction of Union Road and Longmore Road. A local tradition stated that the wood's name derived from the hanging of a highwayman nearby, but it is more probable that 'Grave' is an alternative to 'Grove'.

23.   Longmore Road was originally part of Shirley Heath. The name Longmore means 'the long heath', and was recorded in a deed dated 1426 in the Archer collection (now at Stratford Record Office).

24. By 1930 many new houses were being built in the area to accommodate the influx of new residents. Roads like Longmore Road leading off Stratford Road filled with new houses, and whole new roads such as Burman Road (constructed in 1911) appeared. More roads, such as Jacey Road and Ralph Road, were created in this decade.

25. Marshall Lake Road probably derives its name from John le Machun, who was associated with Shirley in the late 13th century. A pool was once situated near the road, and was recorded in the churchwardens' accounts of 1534 as Machynlak, and as Matchin Lake by 1651. When the Rev. Charles Burd was thrown from his horse and severely injured in 1886, this was still an unmetalled country road flanked with deep ditches.

6. More houses were built in Haslucks Green Road and the population continued to grow. By the late 1930s traffic was also increasing.

27. Solihull Road was originally a field path leading from Stratford Road towards Solihull. It is one of the oldest roads linking Shirley and Solihull.

28. The name Widney means 'willow enclosure', and was given in the 14th century to a sub-manor of Longdon (the manor neighbouring Ulverlei, and the other 'parent' of Solihull). Widney Lane was described in the late 15th century as 'the King's highway leading from Sherley to Shelley'. It was known as Whey Porridge Lane in the 19th century, meaning 'sour, marshy, dirty lane'.

29.   The junction of Tanworth Lane and Stratford Road was known as Red Cow Corner, after a former inn. Tanworth Lane was once a country lane with a few cottages, but now contains many houses. This is the view along Tanworth Lane towards the junction with Stratford Road.

30.   Stanway Road is typical of development which took place in Shirley during the 20th century. This road was once a fordrough (a rough unmade path) across the fields of Shirley Farm, opposite the *Saracen's Head.*

Transport

Stratford Road became a turnpike road around 1725 and was the main route from Birmingham to Stratford and Oxford. A sale catalogue of 1811 called it 'the great London Road'. The *Red Lion* and the *Saracen's Head* were coaching inns; the latter displeased Lady Luxborough in 1747 by refusing hospitality on her journey home to Barrells Hall at Umberslade (although it was 11.00 p.m.!). The tollgate was situated a few yards south of the *Saracen's Head*, with the tollhouse on the opposite side of the road. Thick hedges were planted on either side of the road to prevent travellers circumventing the gate to avoid payment of tolls, but stories survive of ingenious routes around the gate. Tolls ceased in 1872, but the gate itself survived for many years until it was taken to a local farm.

31. After the Turnpike Trust was dissolved, there was still a great deal of custom for the *Saracen's Head*, as it was the terminus for the daily horse-drawn omnibus from Birmingham which had been in service since the 1850s. Trade for the village also came from parties of excursionists from the city in horse-drawn brakes bound for Earlswood Lakes. The road surface was poor and frequently flooded, and in bad weather horses' hooves could slip. Male passengers (and sometimes female too) often had to alight and walk uphill.

SODA
FOUNTAIN

ICED
FRUIT
DRINKS

SELECTA

32.   Horse-drawn transport continued to be used into the 20th century, with most of the public houses providing horse
roughs. Towards the end of the 19th century more leisure time became available for the middle and working classes,
especially on Bank Holidays and Sundays. The Stratford Road, shown here c.1910, became a popular route for city dwellers
seeking fresh air in the country, at first walking and later cycling.

33. Bicycles gave ladies greater freedom to travel. Miss Mabel Wilson, daughter of the landlord of the *Plume of Feathers*, is shown with her bicycle outside the front door in about 1910. Many cycling clubs from Birmingham favoured the route out to Hockley Heath and beyond, along Stratford Road, providing custom for several establishments serving refreshments.

34. By the early years of the 20th century occasional motorcars were appearing in addition to bicycles. This view of Stratford Road is looking from St James' church towards Birmingham. The fields on the left are now the site of the post office, the clinic and the Shirley Centre.

35.   In the years following the First World War petrol stations and cafés appeared along the Stratford Road to cater for the needs of travellers. Noel Boston (writing in *Solihull and its Surrounding District*, published in 1929) described Shirley as 'a straggling village on the Stratford Road ... [which] appears to consist mainly of places of refreshment and garages, indeed it has been called "the village of petrol pumps"'.

36.   By the 1930s garages such as Edmonds' were in much demand. In June 1935 the garage was a Ford specialist but Mr. Edmonds advertised sales and service for any make of vehicle, and car hire was available day and night.

37. Archer's garage was built on the corner of Marshall Lake Road and Stratford Road, opposite the *George and Dragon*. Evans Halshaw now trade on the same site.

38. In the 1930s, Archer's garage had a small café providing refreshments for travellers.

INTERIOR OF CAFÉ, ARCHER'S SERVICE STATION, SHIRLEY

39. By the 1950s, the population of Shirley had increased dramatically, with many more residents becoming car owners. Mrs. Dorothy Webb is shown outside her home in Sandy Hill Road, *c*.1952, using a starting handle to start the family car.

40. Around 1907 the electric tramway from Birmingham was brought to Hall Green, terminating first at the *College Arms*. New technology soon enabled the trams to ascend the hill to the *Bull's Head*. Eventually a new terminus was created at the Hall Green/Shirley boundary near Sandy Hill Road. Plans exist showing a proposal to extend the route down to Shirley, although these were never implemented. Passengers had to walk to the terminus, although some commuters cycled, paying to leave their bicycles in a cottage garden for the day.

41. The Stratford canal passes through Shirley, entering the parish at Solihull Lodge. An Act of Parliament was passed in 1793 to permit the canal to be constructed, linking the Worcester to Birmingham canal at King's Norton with Stratford-upon-Avon, but work was delayed and by 1798 the canal was navigable only to Hockley Heath. It was finally completed in 1816. An aqueduct carries the canal over the river Cole in Solihull Lodge.

42. In the 19th century many barges used the canal, with several firms running regular timetables. Muddiman's coal wharf is shown here in heavy snow when the canal had frozen.

43. After much campaigning by local residents the railway (shown here c.1928) finally came to Shirley in 1908. The station was built in Haslucks Green Road, about a mile to the west of the Stratford Road, and was then in countryside. The first stationmaster was Frank Mutch. Shirley is situated on the line from Birmingham to Stratford-upon-Avon via Henley-in-Arden. This line has been threatened with closure several times since the 1960s.

Churches

44. St James' church (shown here from the Stratford Road gate *c*.1908) was originally built as a chapel-of-ease to Solihull parish church in 1831 by the Rev. Archer Clive, Rector of Solihull, in response to a petition from Shirley residents. The land was given by the Earl of Plymouth, then Lord of the Manor of Solihull and the Rector's cousin. The chapel was consecrated by the Bishop of Lichfield on 2 August 1832. The war memorial now stands inside this gate.

45. The original chapel was a simple building with a tower, nave and apse, and had cost £1,584 to build. It was in the charge of a curate, the Rev. John Griffin (headmaster of Solihull Grammar School). A separate parish was created in 1843. The church appears to have been badly constructed – by 1838 it had dry rot and leaked. Improvements were made in 1862, and it was enlarged in 1882-83 by the addition of a chancel and transepts.

46. A continuous gallery ran around three sides of the original chapel (shown here before the additions of 1882), which contained box pews and a three-decker pulpit. The altar was in an unusual position at the west end. A tradition stated that this was to distance it from the disturbances at the *Plume of Feathers* opposite, but an error in reading the architect's plan is a more probable explanation.

47. The wedding of Denis and Dorothy Webb in November 1955. The chancel had been added in 1882-83, but the altar remained at the west end until the late 1960s when the interior was turned around. Gas lighting was installed in 1886, oil lamps having previously been used.

8. The first vicar appointed in 1843 was Thomas Nash Stephenson, formerly curate at St Alphege, Solihull. He worked hard for his parish, and his efforts were appreciated – the parish marked his marriage in 1857 with two days of celebrations, presenting several gifts and a testimonial praising the vicar's efforts. Stephenson left in 1867 to become vicar of Bromyard, where he died in 1876.

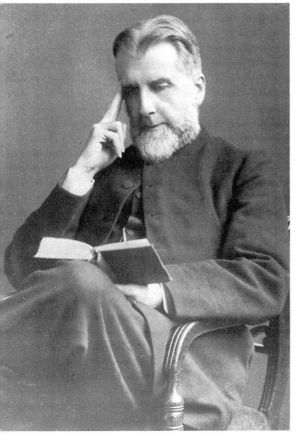

49. Charles Burd, originally from Shropshire and formerly curate at Lapworth, was Shirley's second vicar. He made several improvements during his ministry which included enlarging the churchyard in 1869 and building the extension in 1882-83. He was largely responsible for gas being brought to Shirley in 1886. In July 1900 Mr. Burd collapsed during Evensong one Sunday and died shortly afterwards without regaining consciousness.

50. Charles Ernest Burd succeeded his father as vicar of Shirley in 1900, remaining until 1912. In that year he built Church House, on the site of a cottage opposite the church. His sister Marion was headmistress of Solihull School for Girls. Succeeding vicars included: C. O. R. Wormald (1913-17); C. W. Kerr (1917-22); S. P. Riley (1922-41); J. S. Billings (1941-51); K. W. Breed (1951-77); P. W. A. Whelan (1977-86); and Fr. Michael Caddy, since 1987. All the clergy have contributed to the improvement of church and parish.

51. The first vicarage was built by Archer Clive in 1846 on 3½ acres given by his wife Caroline. It included a stable and coach house (which is now the site of the present vicarage) and pasture for the horses. Archer and the Church Commissioners shared the £1,000 building costs. The Rev. Charles Burd enlarged the house in 1874. In recent years it has been demolished to make way for the Bishopton Close development.

52. A team of handbell ringers at St James celebrating the coronation of King George V and Queen Mary in 1911. In 1855 a public subscription raised £217 to buy four church bells. More followed in 1856 and 1929, with two further bells added as a war memorial after the Second World War. Subscriptions raised £66 for the church clock in 1847, and £65 for a barrel organ in 1849 (replaced in 1862 by a two-manual organ).

NEW BAPTIST CHAPEL AND SCHOOL ROOMS,
SHIRLEY STREET,
FOUR MILES FROM BIRMINGHAM, ON THE STRATFORD ROAD.

On TUESDAY AFTERNOON, AUGUST 19, 1845,
THE NEWLY-ERECTED

BAPTIST CHAPEL & SCHOOL ROOMS
WILL BE

OPENED,
WHEN

SERMONS WILL BE PREACHED
BY THE
REV. THOMAS SWAN, IN THE AFTERNOON,
AND
BY THE REV. JAMES ROBERTS, IN THE EVENING.

ON LORD'S DAY, AUGUST 24, 1845,
SERMONS
WILL BE PREACHED BY THE
REV. C. H. ROE, IN THE AFTERNOON,
AND BY THE
REV. WILLIAM STOKES, IN THE EVENING.

Services will commence each Day at Three o'clock in the Afternoon and at Six in the Evening.

☞ COLLECTIONS WILL BE MADE AFTER EACH SERVICE TOWARDS THE BUILDING FUND.

THERE WILL BE A TEA PARTY ON TUESDAY AFTERNOON, AT 5 O'CLOCK,
IN THE OLD SCHOOL ROOMS. TICKETS, NINE PENCE EACH.

DIVINE SERVICE
Will in future be conducted every Lord's Day, at Three o'clock in the Afternoon and at Six in the Evening.
THE SCHOOLS WILL BE OPEN
For the Admission of Scholars, every Lord's Day Morning, at Ten o'clock, & in the Afternoon at half-past One

Omnibuses will leave the St. George's Office, High-street, Birmingham, on Tuesday Afternoon, for Shirley Street, at Two o'clock. Fare, there and back, 1s. 6d. each.

PRINTED BY J. W. SHOWELL, UPPER TEMPLE-STREET, BIRMINGHAM.

53. Baptist worship began in 1797 when the Rev. Samuel 'Seraphic' Pearce (a minister from the influential Cannon Street chapel in Birmingham) obtained a licence from the Bishop of Lichfield and Coventry to hold services at *The Cock House*. In August 1845 the first Baptist chapel was opened, built by public subscription on the opposite side of Stratford Road.

4. The chapel was a 'village station' with the congregation ~~ill members of Cannon Street chapel (later re-named ~~raham Street church). In 1907, due to the expanding ~~opulation of the neighbourhood, an independent Shirley ~~hurch was formed. A new church, the Guy Memorial ~~aptist church, was opened on its present site in March 1911. ~~ome of the church frontage was lost when a service road was ~~uilt about 30 years ago.

5. The architects of the Guy Memorial church were ~~lessrs. Ingall and Son, and the builder was Mr. Thomas ~~ohnson, all of Birmingham. The church was built of brick ~~ith stone dressings, an open timber roof and a marble ~~aptistry in front of the chancel. It seated about four hundred ~~eople.

56. The foundation stone of the new church was laid on 15 June 1910 by Mrs. R. J. Braithwaite (left on platform) who together with her husband (seated on the left) had given £5,000 to build the church in memory of her parents, John and Marianne Guy. Also seated on the right of the platform are the Rev. J. Walter Young, pastor of Shirley, and his wife. Tea was later served in the tent.

57. In 1901 a gentleman called James Botteley from King's Heath Methodist church gave a plot of land measuring 827 square yards in order to build a Wesleyan Methodist chapel in Shirley. The land on Stratford Road near Solihull Lane had been bought for this purpose. The corrugated-iron chapel opened on 22 September 1903. A Sunday school was founded in 1905.

8. The chapel could accommodate about one hundred and twenty people. It had gas lighting and was furnished with wooden chairs, a harmonium and a reading desk. Shirley was placed under the pastoral charge of Sparkhill Methodist church until 1913, when Mr. Sidney Chapman was appointed as Lay Agent (now called Lay Pastor). The chapel was destroyed by fire (possibly caused by a painter's blowlamp) on 18 June 1929.

59.   The chapel was insured for £1,000, but the increasing population of Shirley necessitated a larger building. Land adjacent to the chapel was purchased and a new church costing £2,279 was opened in May 1930. The fire was eventually seen as a blessing in disguise, despite the work involved. The Chairman of the District once jokingly enquired about the brand of matches the church had used, so that he could supply them to certain other churches!

60.   The building debt was cleared by the end of 1931 and the congregation immediately launched a fund to construct a school. Hall Green Methodist church offered a wooden building which was re-erected at a cost of £250, and officially opened by Miss Dorothy Cadbury on 23 July 1932. In 1941 the church's forecourt was lost when the service road was constructed.

61. Mr. Bertram Smedley (1893-1977), shown here *c.*1914, served Shirley Methodist church in various capacities for over 60 years. He was appointed Lay Agent in 1914, organist in 1925, and also served as Trust Secretary and Chapel Steward. In 1959 he presented a new two-manual organ (which he and Tom Sheffield of Olton had designed) in memory of his parents and first wife.

62. The steadily increasing population necessitated extensions to the church: in 1953 a new hall for the Sunday school was opened, and another extension was added in 1966 (replacing the 'hut') together with a church porch. By the late 1980s the building was totally inadequate, and at the time of writing a new church is under construction and is due for completion in autumn 1993. The drawing below shows the architect's impression of the new building.

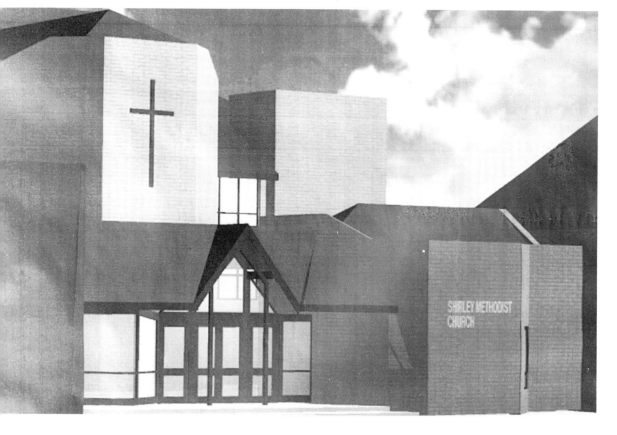

In 1934 Heathfield Convalescent Home, Stratford Road, was purchased for use as a Roman Catholic church. The project was organised by Fr. Rowan from Solihull Catholic church, Fr. Murphy (Yardley Wood) and Dean O'Hagan (Sparkhill). Two rooms were made into one and Fr. Rowan did much of the work himself. The new mission chapel was opened in June 1934 by Monsignor C. J. Cronin, Vicar General of the Birmingham Archdiocese, and dedicated to Our Lady of the Wayside. Reference was made at the service to the 'great movements of population taking place on the outskirts of Birmingham' necessitating the creation of new parishes. This chapel, which seated 200, was intended as temporary accommodation for the Catholic church, and a permanent building was planned, to be constructed in the grounds of Heathfield. The first parish priest, Fr. E. J. Cullen, was appointed in October 1935.

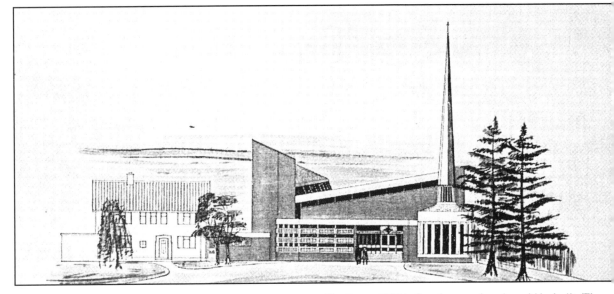

63. It was 1966 before the new church could be built. There was a great deal of discussion on liturgy and theology between Mr. Brian Rush (the architect and a parishioner) and Fr. Patrick O'Mahoney before the plans were completed. Great emphasis was placed on simplicity and light, the aim being 'to make the congregation feel at one with God'. Seating for 700 is arranged in a horseshoe with no-one more than 60 ft. from the altar. The altar, made from seven tons of Portland stone, is the church's focal point.

64. Monsignor Patrick O'Mahoney was parish priest of Shirley for 29 years, during which time he raised over ten million pounds for Third World charities and Human Rights groups. A founder member of Amnesty International, he was appointed to the Pontifical Justice and Peace Commission and served as Chairman of the Birmingham Archdiocese Commission for Justice, Peace and Overseas Development. He was the author of several books and, although working tirelessly to aid the Third World, never lost touch with his parishioners. Fr. Paddy died of cancer on Boxing Day 1991, aged 67. After a Requiem mass at Our Lady of the Wayside he was buried in his home town of Bandon, County Cork.

Schools

65.   The first school in Shirley opened in September 1833, catering only for children under twelve. In 1835 Miss Caroline Meysey Wigley (later Mrs. Archer Clive) gave land for a new building, which was described in *Sketch of Solihull*, published anonymously in 1840 as 'a pretty cottage looking building' with two rooms – boys on the ground floor and girls above, with an adjoining house for the matron. The school was rebuilt in 1852 (as shown in above photograph) with a house for the headmaster adjacent.

66.   Although it had been extended, the original building in School Road was again too cramped by 1965 and the school transferred to its present site in Halifax Road. The old building was demolished in 1972, but the distinctive bell was preserved and may still be seen in the present school.

Church Schools, Shirley.

67. Mr. C. J. Perry, in the centre, was appointed headmaster of St James' school in 1875, remaining in office for 44 years. He was also organist and choirmaster at St James' church for nearly 40 years; both he and his wife (second from right, standing) were remembered with affection by generations of pupils. Mrs. Perry was appointed headmistress of the first infants' school, opened in 1902 in St James' Place next to the churchyard.

68.   A group of girl pupils is celebrating the coronation of King George V and Queen Mary in 1911. The school playground was situated near Bills Farm, and pupils' memories record that chaff from the farmyard used to blow into the playground.

69.   In the 1930s new elementary schools were built at Tidbury Green and Haslucks Green; Sharman's Cross Senior School, shown below, was opened on 22 June 1934. The huge increase in population since the Second World War resulted in several new infant and junior schools. Lighthall secondary school was also built. Falling numbers of pupils in the 1980s and 1990s has resulted in some school closures in recent years, including Sharman's Cross.

70. A typical school photograph shows a class from the 1920s, when Mr. Benson was headmaster. One pupil described the classroom as 'barren', but another said she was never happier at any school she later attended. A typical day started with assembly, with latecomers being caned after the final hymn. Irene Hunt, who attended the school between the ages of 11½ and 14, is shown in the second row from the back, third left.

Farms

The area around Shirley was predominantly agricultural, and was essentially a farming community until the early years of the 20th century. An early 19th-century map of Solihull parish (reproduced as the endpapers) shows several farms in the area, with the village a ribbon development along Stratford Road and surrounded by fields.

The census of 1841 shows seven farmers in the immediate vicinity of Shirley Street, and 11 agricultural labourers. There was little change by 1891, with the census that year recording five farmers and seven agricultural labourers. *Kelly's Directory* of 1905 shows 29 farmers. The soil is mainly sand and clay, with some gravel, and the principal crops grown seem to have been oats, wheat and pasture as most farms were dairy farms.

Farming continued into the 1930s. George Reeves was a typical farmer in the 1920s and '30s – he farmed at Bills Farm, growing potatoes, mangolds, swedes and kale for cattle food and hay and corn. Mr. Reeves had a herd of dairy cattle (he kept British Friesians – an unusual breed at the time) and had two milk rounds stretching from College Road, Moseley, to Solihull Road. Milking began at 5 a.m. and the deliveries on the first milk round were completed before breakfast. Mrs. Reeves kept hens whose eggs she sold to regular customers, and cockerels for sale at Christmas. The farm was self sufficient, with a few fruit trees and a couple of pigs supplying the family's needs, along with home-grown vegetables. Butter and cream were made in the dairy attached to the farmhouse, and Mrs. Reeves also made jams, preserves and home-made wine.

71. Jerrings Hall Farm, shown here in the early 1950s, is a Grade II listed building situated off Tanworth Lane. The name probably derives from the name Gerin, recorded in the area in 1282. The land was owned by the Poole Field family for 250 years. The house was probably extended and rebuilt at different times up until the early 18th century.

72. Abel's Farm, Widney Lane, *c.*1950.

73. Yew Tree Farm was situated in Bills Lane and was listed in the Solihull Parish Tithe Schedule of 1840. By the early 1950s it was empty (as shown here) and it was demolished in 1958. Bills Farm was also located in Bills Lane, near the parish church. The ivy-covered house was double-fronted with a porch and door in the centre, and window shutters which were closed on winter nights.

74. Holloway Farm was situated in Danford Lane until it was demolished in 1960. It was a timber-framed building, and is shown here in the early 1950s. An election poster for Martin Lindsay, M.P. for Solihull from 1945-64, can be seen displayed on the building on the right.

75. Sharman's Cross Farm was in Prospect Lane, near the crossroads at Sharman's Cross Road. The name derives from 'Sheereman' which means 'wooldresser' (a craftsman in the cloth trade). The name was first recorded in 1602. The farm was demolished in 1954. The public house of the same name was built in 1976 on part of the former rickyard (on the opposite side of the road).

76. Longmore Farm, in Longmore Road, was an elegant redbrick house. For many years it was the home of Mr. Anthony Underhill, a farmer, who was also a churchwarden of St James' church, and a Shirley councillor. The house was demolished in the late 1950s.

77. Whitlock's End Farm (shown in the early 1950s) is a Grade II listed building, in the fields south of Bills Lane and north of the Stratford canal. It is a timber-framed building with a brick-front elevation.

78. Many old farm buildings, in addition to farmhouses, survived into the 20th century. These old farm buildings at Whitlock's End Farm were photographed in the early 1950s.

79. Another farm, off Tilehouse Lane, has sometimes been described as Whitlock's End Farm on Ordnance Survey maps. This 17th-century barn was photographed in the early 1950s. The only moated site in Shirley parish is nearby, and may have been the site of the original settlement.

80. Three Maypoles Farm in Dickens Heath Road took its name from the triangle of grass at the junction of Dickens Heath Road and Tithebarn Lane, which was known as the Three Maples corner from a group of trees growing there. The farm was photographed in the early 1950s.

81. Another old barn is shown at Tyburn Farm, Whitlock's End. A tithe barn was recorded here in 1356.

82. Woods Farm is situated in Bills Lane near the right-angle bend in the road. Mr. W. Warwick was living at Woods Farm when he campaigned for the railway to be brought to Shirley in the early 20th century, and the line actually runs close to the house.

83. Baxters Farm was situated near Bills Wood. It was probably a 17th-century timber-framed building, named after a family called Bagster who lived in the area in the 18th century. Lighthall School now stands on the farmland.

84. Haslucks Green Farm in the 1930s.

Houses

85. The Sycamores was a large house standing at the corner of Haslucks Green Road and Stratford Road. For many years it was the home of Mr. Thomas Guy, and is shown here *c*.1903. During the Second World War its cellars were dug out for use as air raid shelters, although the house had been demolished in 1939. The site is now occupied by the Powergen (formerly Central Electricity Generating Board) building.

86.   Manor Cottage, Stratford Road.

87. Shirley House was situated on Stratford Road, near to the junction with Olton Road and close to the former *Cock Inn*. A fine house (later known as Beaconsfield), it was the residence in the 19th century of William Smith Burman, a Birmingham solicitor who drove his smart carriage to his office every day. The front garden had ornate railings and a large tree had grown through them, causing much local interest.

88. Light Hall is a Grade II listed building which was constructed about 1750 by Richard Insull and inherited by his nephew John Burman. The house was built of brick and surrounded by a ha-ha. The original entrance on the turnpike road (now Stratford Road) had an avenue of lime trees leading to the house. Dog Kennel Lane takes its name from the kennels housing a later Burman's pack of hounds.

89. Rose Cottage was the second cottage on the left in Church Road. It was one of a number of new houses appearing in the 1870s.

90. Many cottages and houses were built along the Stratford Road, including 'Swiss Cottage' (on the right) which was near the junction with Tanworth Lane. This view of Stratford Road dates from around 1910. In 1925 Bryant and Tucker, the heraldic embroidery firm, moved to this site.

91. These cottages were situated next to the row of shops on the Stratford Road at the corner of Church Road.

92.   This cottage on Stratford Road dated from the days of the turnpike road. It was demolished in 1962.

93.   Many cottages in the area were built in the late 18th or early 19th centuries, and remained unaltered until after the Second World War. Water usually came from a pump or a well, and there was no mains sewage. This cottage was photographed in Union Road *c*.1950.

94. This house stood at the corner of Longmore Road and Blossomfield Road, and is shown around 1900 when its garden was enclosed with a neat fence.

95. Several timber-framed buildings and old cottages were situated in Haslucks Green Road.

96. A later view of Haslucks Green Road shows typical semi-detached houses built by the end of the 1930s. In 1935 Richard H. Davis (a builder living in Burman Road) advertised new three- or four-bedroomed houses, with garage or garage space, for £450 or £650 leasehold in 'healthy Shirley'.

97. Post-war development of the entire Shirley area has been highly intensive. In the 1950s some interesting projects were undertaken by self-build housing associations. Much of the Shakespeare Manor estate was built in this way, including Dovedale Avenue (shown here during construction), built by the Solihull Progressive Housing Association Ltd. between February 1952 and November 1954.

Inns and Public Houses

98. The *Red Lion* was originally a coaching inn, in existence by 1751 and situated in Shirley Street (then the turnpike road between Birmingham and Stratford). Coroners' inquests were held here, with the stables used as a temporary mortuary. The photograph shows the Peace Day parade passing in July 1919. The inn was partially rebuilt in 1937, demolished in 1965, and replaced by shops and a new public house.

99. The *Saracen's Head* (shown here *c*.1900) was also a coaching inn, and was very close to the Shirley turnpike gate. The inn had extensive stabling, which continued to be in demand after the Turnpike Trust was dissolved, for local hunters, hire of horses and traps and stabling for the horses pulling the horse buses which were a daily service from Birmingham.

0. The *Saracen's Head* was rebuilt in the 1930s and is shown here around 1950. In 1971 over 3,000 people signed a petition save the public house when it was under threat of demolition. Planning permission for a proposed shopping development the site was refused at that time.

1. During the early 19th century the inn yard of the *Plume of Feathers* was often the scene of rowdy events such as cockfights, ll-baiting and prizefights. The Solihull constable's report for 1842 stated that a party of dog fanciers who had been watching dog fight had escaped into the inn. This photograph shows the original building on the left.

102.   In 1923 the *Plume of Feathers* was rebuilt and enlarged. Fortunately it has survived plans for its demolition and is still a public house and steak bar, having been refurbished in 1992.

103.   The *Union* was a beer house on the Stratford Road at the corner of Union Road. In 1936 the licence was surrendered in favour of a new public house, the *Three Maypoles*, which was to be opened in 1938, built on the site of the former cider mill. The former *Union* was finally demolished in the 1950s after being used as a sweet factory and store.

104. The original *George and Dragon* was situated in Blackford Road, with a shop between the public house and the junction with Stratford Road. It was licensed as an alehouse by 1842, and known as the *Green Man* until 1861; it was then called the *Travellers' Rest* until 1881.

5. The *George and Dragon* was rebuilt on the corner of Stratford Road around 1912. It was demolished in the late 1980s and placed by Calendar's restaurant. Shirley was sometimes called the village of five public houses, and an old rhyme celebrates em: 'The *Lion* ate the *Saracen's Head*/And drank the *Dragon* dry,/Turned the *Union* upside-down,/And made the *Feathers* fly.'

106.   The *Crown* was situated along the Stratford Road towards Monkspath. This inn had been remodelled but was also victim of the 1980s when it was demolished and replaced by Jeffersons restaurant following a gallant battle by regular customers to save the public house.

107. A cider mill was in operation at Blackford House from about 1890-1935. In the years around 1860 the house was the home of William Avery Beach, a descendant of Thomas Beach, who had started a small business manufacturing weighing machines. The business later moved to Digbeth where Beach was joined by Mr. Avery. The business they founded is still in existence in the West Midlands, trading as W. & T. Avery Ltd. The cider mill was demolished and replaced by the *Three Maypoles* in 1938; it is now known as the *Pickwick*.

108.   The original *Woodman's Rest* (shown below) was a beer house in Union Road. It was demolished in 1934, and a new hotel with the same name was built on the site. The public house was refurbished in 1987, re-opening in time for Christmas.

Entertainment

109. By 1900 the population of Shirley was increasing, but residents were obliged to provide their entertainment locally due to the lack of public transport. By 1867 social activities included penny readings, tableaux vivants, charades, concerts and lectures – events were held weekly and were well supported. The only room available for meetings was the schoolroom, so a decision was taken to found a village institute. Initially Hope Cottage (opposite the *Red Lion*) was used, but money was raised to build the Institute in Church Road on land given by Mr. Richard Burman.

110. The foundation stone of the Institute was laid by Mr. (later Sir) Alfred Bird in 1903, and the building was soon completed and in use. This photograph shows a variety show, *c.*1916. Much of the social life of the village centred upon the Institute, with whole families taking part in events every weekend. Drama productions were staged by the Katrina Lund Players and The Moseley Institute Players. Tickets for these events were sold by Miss Knight at the post office.

111.   The Shirley Community Association was founded at the end of the Second World War, and a community centre was proposed in 1946. The clubhouse of the Shirley Town Football Club had been requisitioned by the War Department, and after the war it was given to Solihull Council, who agreed to rent it to the Association for temporary use until a permanent centre was built. The photograph shows a dance *c.*1960.

112.   The Community Centre in Gilliver Road was opened in May 1948 after volunteers had renovated the building. It continued to be used until the construction of the Shirley Centre, Stratford Road in 1985, on the site previously occupied by the original police station. The Centre was provided by Solihull Metropolitan Borough Council, and is manned by volunteers from the Community Association. The building was officially opened by H.R.H. Princess Anne on 7 October 1985.

113. Shirley Brass Band, shown here *c*.1921, was founded in 1919 by Mr. Hodesdon, who had learned to play the cornet in the Coldstream Guards. The band is still in existence as Shirley Silver Band. An orchestra was founded in Shirley in about 1934 with Mr. John Woolman as the leading violinist. The orchestra often appeared at the Institute, accompanying soloists in the Sunday concerts.

114. The Brass Band played on many occasions, such as the annual carnival. It is shown here leading a procession past the *Plume of Feathers* and the post office.

115. Shirley recreation ground (now known as Shirley Park) was opened on 10 September 1927 by Dr. Coole Kneale. There was a grand opening ceremony with a procession along Stratford Road. In 1934 the park was extended with an entrance created on the Stratford Road, near the *Saracen's Head*.

116.   Shirley Lido, situated in Haslucks Green Road near Shirley station, opened on 13 June 1936. The architect was Herbert Arnold of West Bromwich. The pool was 100 ft. by 40 ft. and held 72,000 gallons of water which was heated to 70°F (about 21°C), chlorinated and changed continuously. It was decorated with white glazed tiles showing blue racing lines, and had non-slip kerbs, diving and spring boards, chutes and changing rooms.

117.   The many attractions at the Lido included a tea terrace (with Harry Pell's Orchestra in attendance every day except Sunday), a children's paddling pool, attractive gardens and a ballroom which accommodated 250 couples. There was a soda fountain and separate lounges and buffet. The Lido closed in 1939 and was used by the local civil defence services during the Second World War. It subsequently became the headquarters of Simmons & Sons, Ltd, paper and packaging merchants.

118. Shirley Racecourse was situated along the Stratford Road at Monkspath. It opened around the turn of the century, and finally closed in 1953 (having closed between 1939-45). The site is now occupied by Shirley Golf Club. On race days the traffic increased so much that anxious parents kept their children at home.

119. Shirley had its share of sporting clubs and societies. The Football Club team is shown here c.1913. The Rev. Hardcastle, curate of St James' church, had first formed a team c.1899.

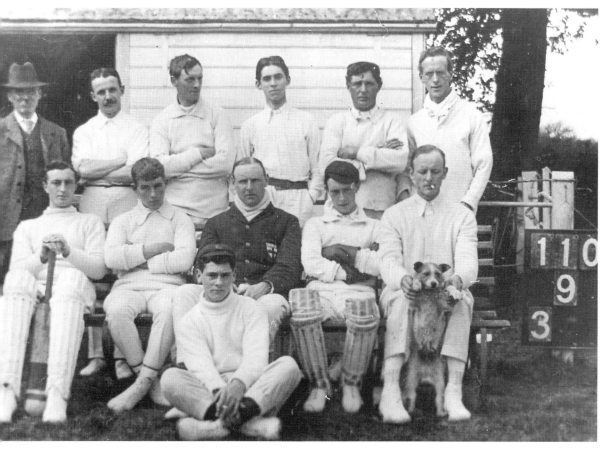

120.   Haslucks Green Cricket Club, *c*.1912. Shirley Cricket Club was founded in 1873 when subscriptions were five shillings per year.

121. Shirley Junior Athletic Club is shown here in 1935-36. Other sporting attractions in the area included skating on frozen flooded fields in Bills Lane, clay pigeon shooting most Saturdays (again in Bills Lane), and the bowling greens at the *Plume of Feathers* and the *Saracen's Head*.

122. Shirley Guides and Scouts in July 1919. Other organisations included the Ancient Order of Foresters, the Women's Institute (founded in 1919), the Horticultural Society and the Residents' Association (established in 1934).

123. Guides and Scouts often took part in the church parade on Sundays. Here they are seen marching along the Stratford Road in the 1930s.

Souvenir Programme

GRAND OPENING OF THE

Odeon Theatre

SHIRLEY

APRIL 15ᵀᴴ, 1935

124. The Shirley Odeon cinema opened in 1935. It was built on fields at the corner of Stratford Road and Solihull Road and was designed to meet contemporary standards and included air purifying equipment. The contractors were B. Whitehouse & Sons Ltd. of Birmingham. The Odeon was later used for some years as a bingo hall, and was finally demolished in 1985. Safeway supermarket now occupies the site.

People and Events

125. Harry Rem (short for Rembrandt) Fowler, winner of the first Isle of Man TT Race in 1907, lived in Shirley for many years. Fowler is shown (second from right) together with J. L. Norton after winning the race in the twin-cylinder class (in spite of suffering from a large abscess on his neck). Riding a Norton motorcycle, his average speed was 36.32 m.p.h. and his lap record 42.91 m.p.h.

126. Rem Fowler retained his interest in motorcycle racing throughout his life. He is seen in this picture with Mike Hailwood (on the left) in 1957. Hailwood's successful career in motorcycle racing included winning 14 TT races and 9 world titles. Hailwood and his young daughter were killed in a tragic road accident near his home in Tanworth-in-Arden in 1981. Rem Fowler died in 1963 aged 81, and is buried in St James' churchyard.

127.   A group of well-known Shirley residents in 1913. Back row (*left to right*): Misses Effie and Winnie Hughes, Mr. Perry (headmaster of St James' school), Miss James, Mr. C. Wyatt, Mr. T. King, Mr. George Bragg; front row (*left to right*): Miss Wakelin, Dr. J. Coole Kneale, The Rev. C.O.R. Wormald (vicar), Mrs. Perry (headmistress of the Infants' school) and Mr. E. Moakes.

128.   The end of the First World War was celebrated with Peace Day in July 1919. This photograph shows the old *Plume of Feathers* decorated for the occasion.

THE PEACE TABLEAU SHIRLEY JULY. 1919.   E MANLEY. EARLSWOOD

129. Everyone participated in the Peace Day celebrations, including the children who presented a tableau and took part in a procession. There was also a lunch for servicemen returned from the war.

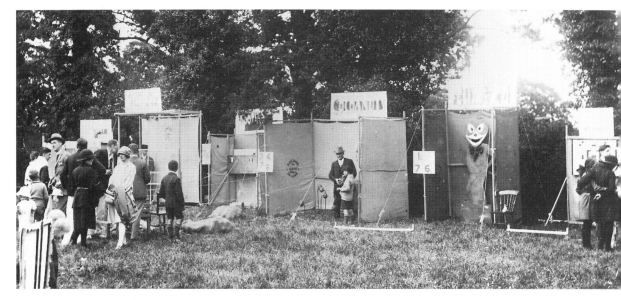

130.   From 1920 a village fête was held in the Vicarage grounds. In 1934 the *Warwick County News* described the fête (held under the auspices of the parish church) as 'the village's most attractive outdoor event of the summer season'. Sergeant Thomas Clark, who was in charge of Shirley police station from 1913, is shown manning the centre stall (a coconut shy) at one of the early fêtes.

131.   Willing volunteers organised the fêtes: attractions included a variety of stalls and sideshows, a nine-hole miniature golf course, sports events and a baby show. In the evening dancing took place in the enclosure, often with special illuminations. In 1934 a firework display provided the grand finale.

132. In 1925 the Midland Motor Cycle Rally met at the remodelled *Plume of Feathers*. Another annual event was the Shirley Horse Show, held before and after the First World War on land behind the *Saracen's Head*, which later became part of Shirley Park.

133. On 10 September 1927 there was a grand celebration to mark the opening of Shirley recreation ground (later Shirley Park). The opening ceremony was performed by Dr. Coole Kneale.

134. Most local organisations joined a procession of decorated floats, led by the Brass Band, and shown here in Stratford Road.

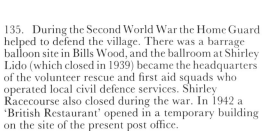

135. During the Second World War the Home Guard helped to defend the village. There was a barrage balloon site in Bills Wood, and the ballroom at Shirley Lido (which closed in 1939) became the headquarters of the volunteer rescue and first aid squads who operated local civil defence services. Shirley Racecourse also closed during the war. In 1942 a 'British Restaurant' opened in a temporary building on the site of the present post office.

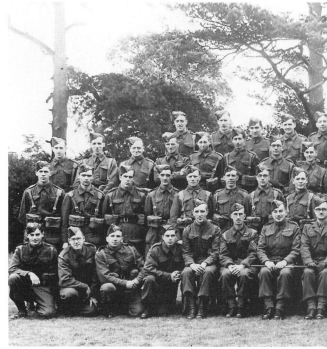

136.   The Home Guard is shown here on parade in Stratford Road, near the junction with Solihull Road. Marching at the front, extreme right, is Councillor H. B. Shaw. Other wartime organisations in the village included the Observer Corps and the Air Raid Precautions Wardens.

137. The first Shirley carnival took place in June 1934 in order to raise money for local charities, including a cot at the Woodlands Hospital, Birmingham. In 1935 the carnival became a week-long celebration, with a carnival king and queen attended by four maids of honour and two jesters. The procession is shown here in Stratford Road in the 1950s. The carnival was abandoned after 1962 but revived in 1980.

138. The actor John Bentley was born in Shirley in 1916. He grew up and was educated in the village. After leaving the stage in 1946 he became the star of the television series *African Patrol*, and later appeared in *Crossroads* and in several films. He visited the carnival in the 1950s, and is shown, on the right, with a friendly 'native'. Vesta Tilley, star of the music hall, and the comedian Sid Field, also lived in Shirley for short periods.

139. In 1954 Solihull was created a municipal borough. H.R.H. Princess Margaret came to present the Charter on behalf of Queen Elizabeth II and the ceremony took place in the Shirley Odeon on 11 March. The Princess (wearing a chocolate brown velvet coat) is shown arriving at the Odeon for the ceremony with Councillor R. D. Cooper, Chairman of Solihull Urban District Council and Mayor designate.

140. Another Royal event occurred on 7 October 1985 when H.R.H. Princess Anne officially opened the Shirley Centre, Stratford Road. The Princess is shown here chatting to the late Tom Bragg about his collection of Shirley memorabilia.

141. For many people, the history of Shirley is inextricably linked with Tom Bragg. Born at Marshall Lake Farm in 1909, he spent his entire life in Shirley, with the exception of military service in the Second World War. Growing up in a rural environment he started work in the building trade, setting up his own business (which included undertaking) in the 1930s. The village Tom had known and loved disappeared under housing developments, but his interest in local history created a collection recording the past. Tom died in December 1992, and is shown here as many will remember him – conducting the funeral of Samuel Kimberlee of the Birmingham Police Force in November 1936.

Trade and Industry

42.   A few shops have existed for many years on Stratford Road near the junction with Church Road. This Edwardian photograph shows a lady cyclist passing the *Plume of Feathers*. Shops included Mr. Knight's butcher's shop and the post office kept by Miss Knight (near right). On 4 May 1940 the roof of the butcher's slid off without warning, having never been fitted properly. The family were having lunch at the time but fortunately no-one was injured.

143. More shops were situated opposite Knight's shop and are shown here in the 1920s. By this time the Plume of Feathers garage had opened.

144. A view of Stratford Road shows the new Baptist church, opened in 1911, on the right. This row of shops included a café on the corner of Haslucks Green Road, and Stokes' hardware shop.

145. Mr. Stokes' Hardware Stores, with Mrs. Stokes standing in the doorway.

146. Shirley Hardware Stores later became Suffields Ironmongers. In 1934 there was a full-page advertisement for the business in *Warwick County News* containing ideas for Christmas. As may be seen, a wide variety of goods was sold in the shop.

147. This 1920s view of the Parade looking towards Birmingham shows newly-constructed shops, with Manor Farm in the distance on the right. Shirley Farm was also situated nearby, opposite the *Saracen's Head*.

148. To meet the needs of the rapidly growing population, many new shops were built after the Second World War. This view (*c*.1960) from the corner of Olton Road shows new shops on the left, with the Parade and Shirley Baptist church opposite. Eventually shops, banks and small businesses occupied most of the Stratford Road from this junction to Marshall Lake Road.

149. During the 1980s the style of the shopping centre began to change, with supermarkets and DIY superstores replacing some of the traditional shops. In 1986 Safeway's store and a branch of the Midland Bank were built on the site of the Odeon cinema. Sainsbury's followed, near the junction with Marshall Lake Road, where there are now several major retail outlets. Tesco's supermarket is located near the M42 junction at Monkspath, next to Nottcutt's Garden Centre.

150. Shirley was an agricultural community, with most of its employment related to agriculture. The blacksmith was very important: at least one was recorded on each of the 19th-century census returns, together with other craftsmen such as wheelwrights, carpenters and bricklayers. This photograph shows Mr. Wood, the blacksmith, on the corner of Longmore Road, still at work in the 1930s.

151.   A number of nurseries and smallholdings were to be found in the settlement. Randalls was once a large employer with a workforce of ten or twelve people, holding land between Longmore Road and Solihull Road. Woolman's Nurseries was another, having moved to Shirley in 1907. This photograph shows Woolman's lorry decorated for the procession celebrating the opening of Shirley recreation ground in 1927. John Woolman received many honours including the Victoria Medal of Honour, one of horticulture's highest awards.

152. Many local weddings had flowers supplied by Woolman's. This photograph shows the bridesmaids at the wedding of Joan and Maurice Garwood in 1953, carrying bouquets by Woolman's. The wedding took place at St James' church where the bridegroom's father, Tom Garwood, was the verger for many years.

153. Many local traders and craftsmen took their services to the customer. Mr. J. Ellis was a mobile knifegrinder for over forty years.

54. As the countryside receded under waves of housing, so businesses increased and diversified; many builders and related services were established, including the plumbers Candy & Morris Ltd. Increases of population also led to a demand for more shops.

55. Light industry included firms like Midland Precision Equipment Co. Ltd. Other firms included Bryant & Tucker (heraldic embroiderers) since 1925, BSA after 1936 and Chemico Works after 1941. Small industrial developments followed, such as the Cranmore Boulevard development. A new research centre opened for Lucas Group in 1965 on a 58-acre site between Dog Kennel Lane and Blackford Road. As has been noted previously, C.E.G.B. (now Powergen) opened a large office block at the corner of Stratford Road and Haslucks Green Road in 1967.

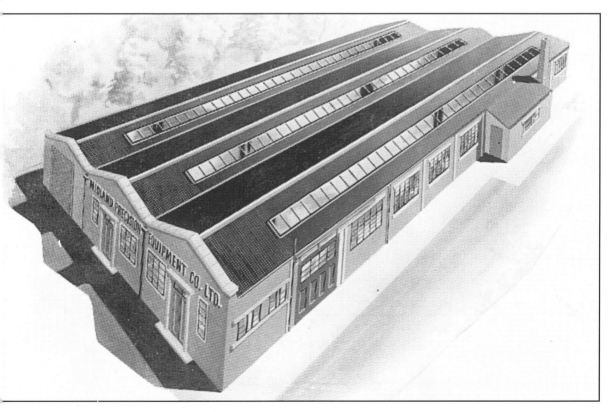

156. Job Wragg's soda syphon is an example of goods manufactured in the area.

157. Exports from Shirley travel all over the world, as these workers in the 1950s discovered. In the 1980s a new business park opened at Monkspath as part of the Cranmore-Widney development.

Solihull Lodge

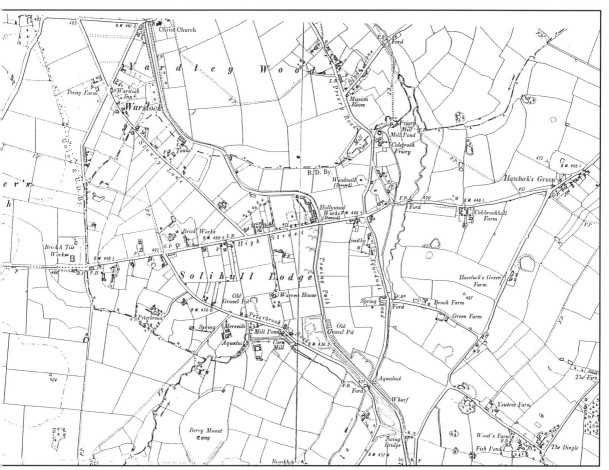

158.   Solihull Lodge extends west of Stratford Road from Haslucks Green. This extract from the second edition of the Ordnance Survey 6 in. to 1 mile map shows the area in 1905. The origin of the name is uncertain; one theory states that there may have been a hunting lodge situated here – the area was wooded and was an open common until enclosure in the early 19th century. Berry Mound, an Iron-Age hillfort, is to the south of Peterbrook Road, just beyond the present borough boundary.

159. The historian John Burman thought the origin of the name may have dated from 1243 when the boundary of Ulverlei was adjusted at this point, giving the manor a portion of land (or 'lodgement') from the adjoining Crown lands in Worcestershire. The settlement of Solihull Lodge consisted of houses situated along High Street, and isolated farms and cottages. These cottages, shown *c.*1900, were on the way to Yardley Wood.

160. Pear Tree Farm was once a beer house called *The White Lion.* Deeds of the house were said to date from the 14th century. The photograph shows a Birmingham Fire Insurance plate on the front of the house.

161. Colebrook Priory is a timber-framed 17th-century house. There is no documentary evidence of a religious establishment on this site, and the house may have acquired the name in the 19th century – it was known by this name by 1871. There are several stories of ghosts associated with the Priory and nearby houses. A grass-covered mound of earth in the grounds has been called a 'praying mound'.

162. Near Colebrook Priory was a large mill pool, formed by damming a stream near to its confluence with the river Cole.
The pool served a water mill originally called Bache Mill, but later renamed Colebrook Priory Mill (shown here *c.*1913). The
mill was recorded in the 15th century, and was working as a needle mill in the 19th century.

163. A windmill was built near the mill pool in the late 18th century. It was a brick tower mill which was enlarged in the 19th century. The windmill was built by the Kendrick family, who operated it until 1880, when the Woollaston family took over Colebrook Priory and both mills. The windmill ceased working around the turn of the century, and was demolished (by explosion) in 1957 to make way for a housing estate.

164. Joseph Else (a steam miller), shown here in his garden, was working Peterbrook Mill by 1884. He was recorded as a widower, aged 75, in the census of 1891, and was living with his son John (who was named as the miller in *Kelly's Directory* of 1900) and daughter-in-law, Sarah.

PETERBROOK RD. YARDLEY WOOD

65. A view of Peterbrook Road shows the bizarre house owned for a time by a well-known local personality, Stanisbury
ardley, who was a lawyer practising in Birmingham. Peterbrook Mill can be seen on the left, built at the side of the mill pool
n Peterbrook stream.

DRAWBRIDGE, SHIRLEY,
–ON YARDLEY WOOD CANAL–

166.   The Stratford-on-Avon canal passes through Solihull Lodge. The drawbridge provided opportunities for local children to earn pennies by raising the bridge for courting couples boating on the canal. The Drawbridge Stores has been replaced by the present public house *The Drawbridge*. By 1965 the old drawbridge proved inadequate for the traffic passing over it and was replaced by a new steel bridge specially made at Gloucester and brought by canal.

67. The canal crosses the river Cole on a high aqueduct. This postcard, dated 1905, shows the river Cole in Aqueduct Lane, with local children who often fished for minnows here. On occasion the canal has overflowed, as, for example, in 1900 when there was extensive flooding over a large area near the aqueduct, leaving the animals at Brookhouse Farm standing in water up to their necks.

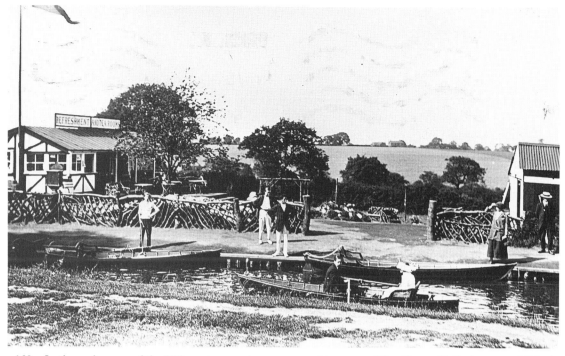

168.   In the early years of the 20th century, a pleasure ground known as 'The Happy Valley' was established alongside the canal. Several postcards exist showing campers, including this view of *c.*1914, waterside tearooms and boating.

169.   The canal also offered opportunity for industry. James Fern Webster constructed his Crown Aluminium Works beside the canal in 1887. This was claimed to be the first commercial production of aluminium in the world, as previous methods had been too expensive to make commercial production viable. Webster died in 1904 and the factory was demolished in 1911.

170. Webster was a self-made business man, and a prolific inventor. His Crown Aluminium Works attracted a great deal of interest. Lord Salisbury (then Prime Minister) was a shareholder and a frequent visitor to the factory, with his nephew Arthur Balfour. Webster is shown here (centre, wearing a light coloured hat and waistcoat) in a Masonic outing from Atholl Lodge, King's Heath in 1889. He died on 1 November 1904, aged 84, and was buried in the family vault at St James' church.

Monkspath

171. The southward stretch of Stratford Road after Marshall Lake Road is traditionally known as Monkspath Street. Strictly speaking Monkspath was not part of Shirley parish, but is included here because it is linked with Shirley. It has been suggested that the name Monkspath (first recorded in 1153) referred to a route between Bordesley Abbey and Merevale Abbey, but there is no documentary evidence to support this theory. This view shows the Stratford Road at Breakwell's, looking towards Lodge Farm in the distance.

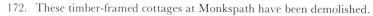

172. These timber-framed cottages at Monkspath have been demolished.

173. Shelley Farm is a timber-framed Grade II listed building dating from the late 16th century, with later brick additions. It has recently been converted into a public house in the centre of the Cranmore-Widney development. The settlement of Shelley was recorded in the Middle Ages, and was partly in Tanworth parish.

174. The Mount Dairy Farm was a redbrick farmhouse built in Tanworth Lane.

175.   Farming at Shelley continued until the early 1980s, when the large housing development stretching from Monkspath to Hillfield and Widney Manor was constructed. This photograph shows haymaking in the early 20th century. Part of an ancient hay meadow survives adjacent to Nottcutt's Garden Centre and has been designated a Site of Special Scientific Interest. The rest of the meadow was moved to another site in an attempt to preserve the rare plants, which have never been chemically treated.

DAIRY FARM

176.   Mount Cottage Farm was situated in Creynolds Lane next to the moated site known as 'The Mount', in the area usually called Cheswick Green, about half a mile south-west of Stratford Road. An archaeological excavation was carried out in the 1950s which concluded that the earthwork was probably constructed *c.*1300 and abandoned after a short period (possibly at the end of the Wars of the Roses). Most of the Mount is now covered by a housing development.

177.   In the early 20th century pleasure grounds were opened at the Mount by Philip Baker, a solicitor. Attractions included refreshments, dancing, swingboats, tennis courts, a bowling green and pierrots. The grounds seem to have had difficulty in attracting sufficient visitors (although groups would come out from Birmingham on fine weekends) and they closed around 1913. Following the First World War a settlement of smallholdings grew up at the Mount, with dwellings consisting of bungalows and chalets. The allotments and dwellings were eventually demolished to make way for the housing development of Cheswick Green.

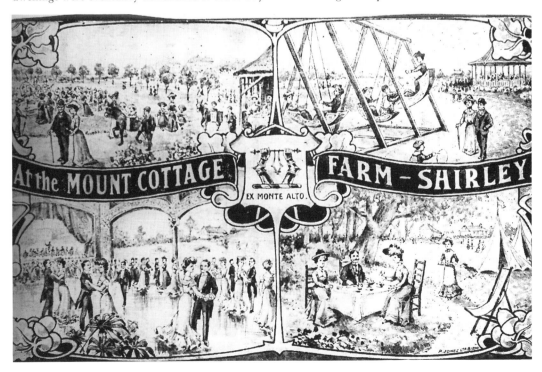

At the MOUNT COTTAGE FARM - SHIRLEY
EX MONTE ALTO.

Bibliography

Burman, J., *Gleanings from Warwickshire History* (1933)
Burman, J., *In the Forest of Arden* (1948)
Burman, J., *Old Warwickshire Families and Houses* (1934)
Burman, J. (revised K. Breed), *Shirley and its Church* (1968)
Causer, M. E., *Study of Stratford Road, Shirley 1905-75*
(unpublished thesis, Bordesley College of Education [*c.*1975])
Census Returns, 1841-91
Clive, M., *Caroline Clive* (1949)
Kelly's *Directories of Warwickshire*, between 1835-1940
Shirley Baptist Church, *Shirley Baptist Church 1797-1972* (1979)
Shirley Women's Institute, *History of Shirley* (1950s)
Shirley Women's Institute, *Shirley Scrapbook* (1960s)
Smedley, B., *Shirley Methodist Church*
Smedley, D., *Shirley Methodist Church* (unpublished thesis 1991)
Solihull News (formerly *Warwick County News*) 1930-to date
West Midlands Federation of Women's Institutes, *The West Midlands Village Book*
(1989)
Wheatcroft, G.W. (née Reeves), *The Shirley I knew* (unpublished typescript, 1984)
Woodall, J., *The Book of Greater Solihull* (1990)
Woodall. J., and Varley, M., *Looking Back at Solihull* (1987)
Woodall, J., and Varley, M., *Solihull Place Names* (1979)